The pen is mightier than the slide

All you need to make your training, facilitation and presentations more engaging by using flip charts

By

Donna McGeorge

First published in 2014
Copyright © 2014 Donna McGeorge
www.donnamcgeorge.com

National Library of Australia Cataloguing-in-Publication entry:

Author:	Donna McGeorge 1966 –
Title:	The Pen is Mightier than the Slide: All you need to make your training, facilitation and presentations more engaging by using flip charts
ISBN:	978-1-304-75994-8
Subjects:	Training
	Presenting
	Drawing
	Visual Thinking
	Communication

Illustrations and layout by Donna McGeorge with the exception of page 41 which has a drawing by Brandy Agerbeck from Loosetooth.com and is used with permission.

Cover design by Matt Emery (www.mattemery.com.au)

For Steve

Unconditional love
Unswerving faith
Unbelievable support

Table of Contents

Chapter 1	What is so bad about PowerPoint?	7
Chapter 2	Why are flipcharts more effective?	13
Chapter 3	What you need for a basic starter toolkit	19
Chapter 4	Skill fundamentals	27
Chapter 5	Getting started	57
Chapter 6	Practice makes perfect	61
Chapter 7	In conclusion	85
Acknowledgements		89
References		90

Chapter 1

What is so bad about PowerPoint?

I don't hate PowerPoint I just think it's misused.

Why? Most people are unaware of the true purpose of PowerPoint and therefore unable to use it to its true potential. I believe this lack of understanding is the number one reason audiences become disengaged before presenters even open their mouths.

Here's a brief history lesson. Before PowerPoint we had slide projectors hence the term "slides" in PowerPoint.

Slides were first used when a speaker or lecturer wanted to show pictures. Rarely, if ever, were there words used on slides. If lecturers or presenters wanted words, they wrote them on a black or chalkboard, flip chart and in some cases a white board.

Along came the overhead projector with film that you wrote on with special markers, to project onto a screen or wall. Some institutions were still using these well into the 2000's. In my view, this heralded the beginning of the end for engaging learning and presentation environments.

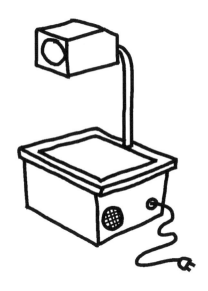

Why? Because then came ink jet printers and special (porous) film that could be put through the printers so you could print your material and project it.....and thus the birth of the misuse of PowerPoint.

Designed as a presentation tool, PowerPoint was never meant to be a word processor. We had, and continue to have, Word for that. Sadly, many use PowerPoint as a word processor and simply project documents onto a screen, overloaded with content and graphs/tables that are so small as to be un-readable.

Unfortunately, many organisations believe that a meeting cannot take place, an idea cannot be expressed or skill be taught without a "deck" of slides. And why is that, do you think? Security blanket? Confirmation of knowledge transfer? Reduced attendance at meetings ("I'll send you the deck")? Covering your $%#@ ("it was in the deck")?

So ... I don't hate PowerPoint, I just think it's misused.

So when CAN you use PowerPoint? Many presentations would be more engaging if they contained more pictures and fewer words. I think it's also useful for one-page summaries, provided it's not just a page full of very small writing.

I spent a couple of years working in China, with many audience members who had English as a second language. Many times PowerPoint was necessary for the audience to follow along, AND YET... when I went to the chart, and wrote or drew a picture, they were more engaged.

SO ... If you want to continue using PowerPoint and would like some great ideas on how to make your PowerPoint slides more effective, take a look at Nancy Duarte's book, Slide:ology.

In the meantime ... you might like to consider an alternative.

Chapter 2

Why are flip charts more effective?

It's about **credibility** and **co-creation**.

Credibility

After over 20 years of presenting to, training and facilitating adults, I have rarely, if ever, used PowerPoint. As a consequence, I commonly get feedback on how much they enjoyed a learning environment without slides. "Refreshing" "Engaging".

And yet, the number one misconception or push-back I get from presenters and trainers when I'm teaching this concept, is that they will be seen as unprofessional if they don't use slides.

What is more unprofessional?

Overloaded slides, no one can read, in a dimly lit room

yawn

OR

A subject matter expert, speaking from their heart and mind, drawing their ideas on a chart.

One is "ho hum", the other is

wildly credible

One of the smartest women I have worked with, who is SUCH a subject matter expert, nearly fainted when I suggested she delivered her content without slides. I pushed, cajoled, coached and eventually she did it. And delivered an amazing workshop.

Make no mistake, when you are able to deliver your whole session on flip charts, you will appear more **credible** and **knowledgeable** on your topic. ANYONE can read a slide. Only an expert can draw and explain their model, thinking, or ideas on a chart, on the fly.

Trust yourself, your experience and your knowledge. Step out from behind the slide and show the world what you are made of.

> # When misused, PowerPoint is the security blanket of the poorly prepared presenter or trainer.

Co-creation

What I have observed over the years is that people like flip charts because it is a co-creative process. By using flipcharts we are inviting participants to contribute.

If I have a set of slides, I have preordained what people will "learn" today. My experience of adults (and to some extent children) is that they don't like to have things preordained and will rebel.

PEOPLE LIKE TO THINK THEY HAVE CHOICES.

So when we deliver our material and create charts with the group, they can **see themselves** in the material through words they have said, concepts that resonated, the story they have related to. They are visual anchors for learning that cement concepts and meaning to their experience.

Not only that, when we progressively post the charts around the room, the participants can see their work, the story and the learning unfold. Both the participants and trainer/facilitator/speaker can then refer to the charts at any time throughout the session.

It's nearly impossible to "jump around" with the content when you are using Power Point. Slides are in a particular order and unless you are a super user and know how to elegantly move around slides (and not many people do), it can be quite disorienting for participants when you jump around, or flick quickly through a deck to get to a particular slide.

With flip charts, you can deliver your content in the order that suits the group, there and then, in the moment.

So....are you convinced? Good! Let's move on!

Chapter 3

What you need for a basic starter toolkit

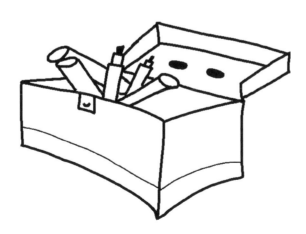

Markers

From now on, and for the rest of your life, you need to **obsess about your markers.**

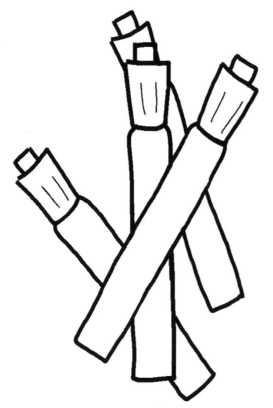

I **never** rely on venue markers because, irrespective of your medium, you will generally be provided with whiteboard markers. Usually bullet tipped, old, dried up and faded. Even if they are brand new out of the box, they won't last ten words on paper because paper is porous and soaks up the ink. Great for whiteboards not flip chart paper.

So you may be asking, "what is a bullet tip?" Bullet tips are rounded and create only one type of line – usually thin.

What we want for great flip charting, is a **chisel tip** pen. They are squared off or angled and give you many different line types.

My favourite chisel tip markers for flip charting are:

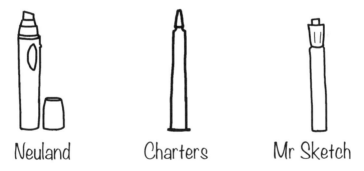

Neuland   Charters   Mr Sketch

Check out the references and resources section of the book for where to buy markers.

BLACK is the best colour for writing on flipcharts simply because it can be seen clearly from a distance.

My actual favourite colour is orange, however orange is one of those colours that literally disappears off a page if the light is shining on it in a certain way.

Save your colours for headings, bullet points and illustrations.

Tip: When buying a set of markers, buy extra black ones. Neuland and The Grove (Charters) allow you to purchase selected markers in individual colours.

Paper & Stand

For the most part, you will simply use the flipchart paper provided at a venue, attached to the stand.

It's also ok to pre stick paper around the walls, depending on your event. You can also pre-prepare charts and hang them, if that's what your content or session demands.

I frequently request two flipchart stands at the front so I can work from side to side, allowing complementary content to be viewed simultaneously until it's placed up on the wall.

If appropriate, at the breaks, hang each of the charts so that the story of your session can unfold for the participants. My suggestion is to keep things neat and aligned. If you have a lot of charts, you can hang them in two rows.

It's up to you if you want choice with your quality of paper. Many of us go along with whatever a venue or employer provides. If you have choice, look for coated paper. Your pen colour will be more vibrant and the paper doesn't suck the life from your markers.

One thing you do want to check is whether the markers you are using will "bleed" or go through the paper. There are not many venues that will thank you for leaving ink all over their walls! If you are using new paper and new markers that you are not familiar with, check this thoroughly before mounting any paper on walls.

What else?

In addition to paper and pens, I carry the following in my toolkit so that I am always prepared for any eventuality:

☐ Grey lead pencils to make notes on your chart no-one can see, or to sketch a picture or an idea before committing to ink

☐ Eraser

☐ Address labels in case you make a mistake and you can just stick one right over the top of it

☐ Post it notes for activities or to quickly capture things to put on the chart later

☐ Sticky dots for any voting activities

☐ Image binder or tablet to access to your own collection of favourite images or icons

☐ Digital Camera, or phone/tablet to capture your charts

☐ Small packet of tissues for a runny nose, or if you are using chalk pastels for subtle shading or that "air brushed" effect

☐ Paper cutter to cut either lengths of paper or if the flipchart paper provided is not perforated. I have found a great paper cutter that is appropriate to take in your carry on when flying. It's called a "gift paper cutter", made by Scotch.

☐ Water bottle so you stay hydrated

☐ Aspirin, paracetamol – for you and if pain persists...see your doctor!

☐ Tape/BluTack

☐ Box cutter/scissors in case supplies have been delivered directly to the venue (when flying, only if I have checked luggage)

Tip: I have two basic sets always ready to go containing markers, BluTack, post it notes, pencil and eraser so that if I am doing multiple sessions back to back, I know I always have a full kit ready to go.

Chapter 4

Skill Fundamentals

Handwriting

It's your number one skill and yet so few of us practice this. Your handwriting needs to be

- Legible
- Repeatable
- Fast

And these **ARE** in order.

Legible - Think colour and size.

As mentioned earlier, the best colour for handwriting is BLACK, however any of the darker colours would be ok, for example dark or navy blue, brown and dark green. Avoid orange, red, lime green, light blue or yellow for anything other than headings or features (bullets, drawings, etc).

<u>Size</u> must be read from a distance. After all it is for your audience that you are writing.

It needs to be at least 3cm in height. →3

You can always do a practice chart and go to various parts of the room (before the audience arrives) and see if you can read the writing from every corner.

Repeatable - What is your handwriting **font**?

Decide to have one and work on it. Something you can practice and develop over time. Some things to consider:

- Upper or lower case? There was a time when I had very strong views about this but I have mellowed somewhat. In the past I followed the example of the most read items in the world -

newspapers. Generally their headings were upper case and text or body was lower case. I'm guessing newspapers have "readability" experts whose job it is to make text as readable as possible. I figured I'd follow their example.

The rationale against using all upper case is that letters are all the same size and tend to "block" meaning the reader's brain has to work a little harder at reading them. Lower case letters are different sizes making it quicker to identify words.

ABCDEF
GHIJKL
MNOPQR
STUVWX

If you are doing typed work, I would go along with this. With handwriting, however, the general inconsistency will work in your favour.

Nowadays I still typically use upper case for headings and lower case for the rest of the chart, and I do know of some people who do all of their handwriting in upper case and it looks just fine.

- Oval or round? It doesn't matter as long as you stick to one or the other. In this example, the first two lines are examples of oval and the third and fourth lines are round.

ABCDEFGHIJKL
abcdefghijklm
ABCDEFGHI
abcdefghijkl

- Thick or thin? This will depend on what part of the marker you are using. The nib, or the whole chisel length. This also comes down to readability from a distance.

ABCDE abcde
ABCDE abcde

IT'S ALL ABOUT CONSISTENCY

I prefer holding the chisel between 10 and 11 o'clock and using the whole nib length.

Looking down the length of the (chisel tip) marker along the longest part of the nib would be considered 12 o'clock.

Turning the marker slightly to the left, so the longest part of the nib is pointing to about 10 o'clock is my preference. For me it gives just the right size, shape and density.

Are you left handed? Hold the pen at about 2 o'clock.

A professional sign writer told me once that, with upper case, its best to do vertical strokes first, then horizontal. It creates a more even and consistent font.

And again for consistent strokes, don't go over the same line twice. Sometimes when drawing an A or an M, we might do the first down stroke, and without lifting the pen, go up again (over that same stroke) to draw the second down stroke, and so on..

Lift the pen completely and draw, in the case of an A, three distinct strokes and in the case of an M, four strokes.

With lower case, we frequently need to go over the same line, or section of line so no need to worry about this.

Fast

As a front of room professional, I regularly need to capture content...fast! Participants call out ideas and they don't have time or patience for me to capture slowly. So you need to have handwriting that is legible, repeatable and FAST.

Practicing the first two will lead to the third. Once you begin to use flipcharts on a daily basis this will take care of itself. In the meantime, see the section later in this book with drills and activities that can help you with this.

Headings

My suggestion is that you write all your headings the same **colour** so that when your charts are up on the walls, a person can skim along the top, reading the heading and get the "gist" of your material. Well selected headings will tell a short story.

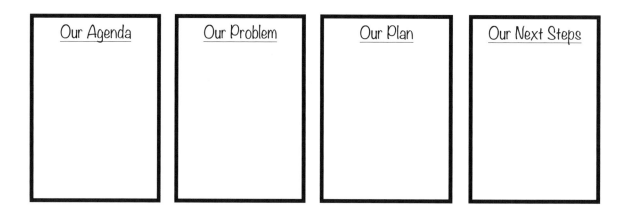

Pick a colour at the beginning of the day and stick with it. My favourite is red.

With headings, pick a **style** and technique. This will depend on how much time you have. No group wants to stand around while you are creating elaborate headings, no matter how artistically they are executed.

So you could just do a heading

Then underline it

If you have more time, make a box

If you have plenty of time or are well practiced, make it a banner (see page 45 for how to draw banners)

It's also ok to pre-write your headings at the beginning of the session giving you plenty of time to do whatever heading style you like.

Drawing people

It's said that a picture paints a thousand words. Most of the work we do as presenters, trainers and facilitators involves people. If you can draw a basic shape to represent people, you can make more meaning for your audience. Here are some very basic ways of representing people.

When it comes to drawing people, know your limitations, and stretch. For example if your limitation is a stick person, then stretch by adding shoulders, hips, hands and feet.

For examples of taking your drawings to new levels, check out the resources section of this book for visual dictionaries and other "how to" books.

In the beginning, you might like to pre-draw your pictures, or draw them in pencil on your charts first so they appear that you are drawing in the moment. As you become more comfortable with these techniques, you will find you don't need to pre-prepare. Particularly as you develop and grow your visual vocabulary.

Drawing general icons

There are some basic universal icons that can be used for representing ideas or concepts. Build up your own visual vocabulary by practicing these basics and then looking for more. Take a look at Google images and search for words and look for common themes. This helps when looking for simple icons for complex ideas.

See the visual vocab section for instructions for drawing each of these and more.

You don't need to be an artist. You are simply using lines and shapes cleverly (quote from a previous participant).

So don't go over the top.

Remember, it should be content first. Get the participants' words first before worrying about drawings or, as my good friend and colleague Brandy "the draw" Agerbeck always says....
"CONTENT IS KING"

Brandy Agerbeck, Loosetooth.com

Bullets, boxes, banners and borders

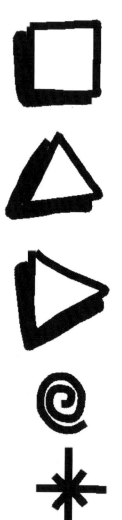

Bullets

Speed is of the essence here. You haven't got all day so make a call early in your event about what bullet styles you will use.

After speed, it's about consistency. Choose a couple of style levels, for example level one bullet points could be a drop shadow, and level two (or sub bullets) are a dash or asterix.

My favourite is the dropped shadow box.

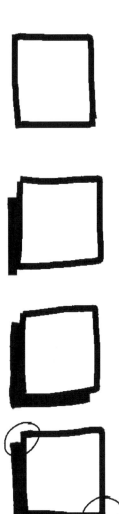

1. Draw a box

2. Starting just down from the top of left vertical draw a line next to the box with the thickest part of the pen.

3. Then on the bottom horizontal draw a thick line again, finishing just before the end of the box.

4. The trick is making sure you don't go all the way to the ends to create the "dropped" shadow effect

Boxes

A very experienced graphic recorder once said to me "words first, then the box". I know this seems obvious, but consider the alternative...

Banners

These make any heading look more impressive. There are a couple of ways of drawing them.

1. Words or heading first
2. Then a box
3. Then add a W and M to each end of the box as follows making sure you use sharp (not rounded) tips.
4. Close up the ribbon and the corner.

You can make them curved as well.....

And really flow.....

Borders

I once heard that anything with a box or border around it would draw the eye. Take a look at the following identical lists. Which one draws your eye?

Agenda

- ☐ Introductions
- ☐ Minutes from previous meeting
- ☐ Agenda Item One
- ☐ Agenda Item Two
- ☐ Agenda Item Three
- ☐ Agreements
- ☐ Next Steps
- ☐ Wrap up

Agenda

- ☐ Introductions
- ☐ Minutes from previous meeting
- ☐ Agenda Item One
- ☐ Agenda Item Two
- ☐ Agenda Item Three
- ☐ Agreements
- ☐ Next Steps
- ☐ Wrap up

Now, take a look at this large scale chart. It is a "practice" chart showing several different techniques we have already discussed in this book. When you look at this example, where is your eye drawn?

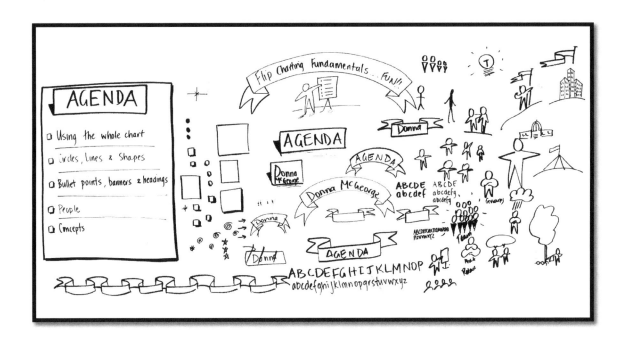

Borders can be basic or elaborate. I would go for consistency and it's fun to break them up over words or pictures to be a bit more dynamic. Using a thicker pen like a Neuland BigOne ® marker is great for a border.

Use models to make meaning

There are four fundamental ways in which we can represent our words or concepts as pictures:

X & Y Axis or 4 Boxer

Polarity

Venn Diagram

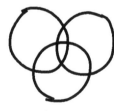

Triangle

For example, who do you want on your team?

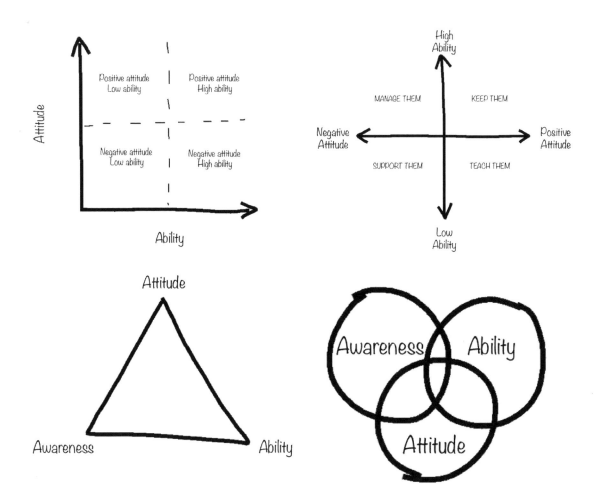

Top left quadrant chart:

Attitude (vertical axis) / Ability (horizontal axis)

- Positive attitude / Low ability
- Positive attitude / High ability
- Negative attitude / Low ability
- Negative attitude / High ability

Top right quadrant chart:

High Ability / Low Ability (vertical) — Negative Attitude / Positive Attitude (horizontal)

- MANAGE THEM
- KEEP THEM
- SUPPORT THEM
- TEACH THEM

Bottom left triangle:

Attitude / Awareness / Ability

Bottom right Venn diagram:

Awareness / Ability / Attitude

Any of these models could be used to express your idea, and the best thing to do is experiment to find the right one for you.

Knowing which one to use in the moment comes with experience, and a simple way to think about it is by the number of ideas or concepts being discussed, eg:

2 concepts – x/y axis or polarity model
3 concepts – triangle
3 or more – venn diagram

What I have discovered in my use of such models is that when you are able to present your thinking, the problem, or the discussion being had in a very simple visual way, people generally respond with a resounding "Yes! That's it EXACTLY!"

Makes you look very smart!

Capturing brainstorms or group call outs

The essence here is speed. The group won't have the tolerance (nor should they) for you to spend too much time being artistic. Here are three great ways to capture information that is still quick, but adds a bit of zing to the page. These are generally used when gathering information "popcorn" style, which is random placement on the page, rather than an ordered list.

Post it Notes

Speech Bubbles

Thought Bubbles

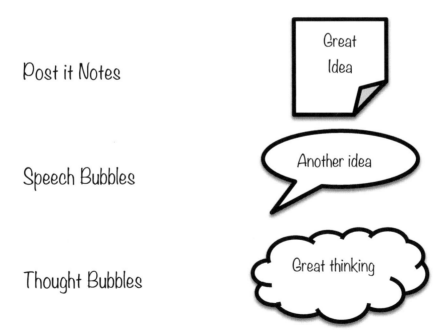

Taking an even BIGGER step

Many of my colleagues who work with pen and paper do it on a large scale, referring to themselves as scribes, graphic recorders and graphic facilitators, amongst other things. Once you have mastered flip charts, consider presenting your content on a large sheet or whiteboard. Here are some of my personal examples of delivering and capturing content on large sheets of paper.

This is a chart I pre-prepared for a world café session I was facilitating.

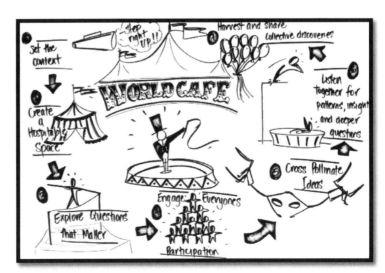

This chart was for my daughter who was studying Russian history and struggling with remembering dates and details. I asked her to talk me through her notes, and while she spoke, I captured the information on a large chart. She later told me that during her exam, she was able to visualise the chart on the wall, and the details contained which helped her to get a great result.

This last chart is an example of delivering content for a one-day workshop. The participants were quite young (in their early 20s) and at the end a number of them said that the chart helped to keep them engaged in the content. Sorry, had to black out the client name.

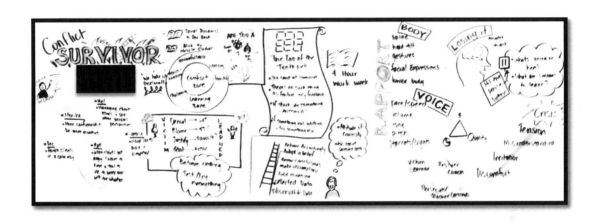

3 things to consider when going large

1. **Space** - I can generally produce a whole day of content on a 3 metre chart but you will need to plan and rehearse *or* pencil in major parts to keep the chart balanced.
2. **Right to left or centred** - like space above, think about how you will lay out the content.
3. **Style guide** - choose no more than 4 colours. Decide headings, sub headings bullets and font sizes in advance so you don't have to waste any chunks of attention. (Chunks? See the next chapter).

Again, pick a topic that you know well for the first attempt and have plenty of spare paper, including flip charts in case you run out of space.

 Sign and date your work and be prepared for photographs.

Chapter 5

Getting started

If you are thinking about cutting ties with PowerPoint, choose a topic you are VERY familiar with to flip chart giving you a spare chunk or two of attention to work with.

What do I mean by "chunk of attention"? George Miller, in the 1960's, came up with the magic number of 7 +/- 2 representing the amount of information (or chunks) we can hold in our conscious minds. It's why we can only remember a certain amount of items (or chunks) on a shopping list, or why we get overloaded (or over-chunked) in complex learning environments, or why we can feel overwhelmed (or over-chunked) when we have too many things to do.

So, pick a topic where you have some spare chunks of attention to do something a little different.

- Pre-prepare a welcome chart. If it's a small group, use their names on it. It's a nice touch.

- Gather "outcomes or objectives or experiences" visually

- Gather a brainstorm and put speech bubbles or post it notes around each item.

-
- Decide to do one thing consistently. For example banner headings, single colour headings, bullets, upper or lower case writing, border, adding a visual.
- Pre-prepare some of your headings and write some of your content in pencil on the sides of the chart as prompts.

By now, you should have enough to get started. The following pages contain some drills and practice activities for you to begin to hone your ability.

Chapter 6

Practice makes perfect

Drills

The following activities are designed for you to get comfortable up at the chart and to build your flip charting muscles. So, grab a flip chart stand or put some paper on the wall, pick up a pen and have some fun.

Circles- Hold the pen in your fist, like a sword and stand an arms length from your chart and relax, moving your arm from the shoulder, draw large circles. If you are doing this right, you should get pretty good balanced and consistent circles.

> Your body knows how to draw. Your mind gets in the way

Drop lines - hold the pen like you are going to write as normal. Imagine there is a weight connected to your wrist and you are fighting against it. Put the nib of the pen on the top of the page, and then succumb to the weight. Let the pen and your wrist drop, drawing a straight line on the page. Repeat this several times. If you are doing it right, you should get fairly straight vertical lines that are heavy at the top and taper off at the bottom.

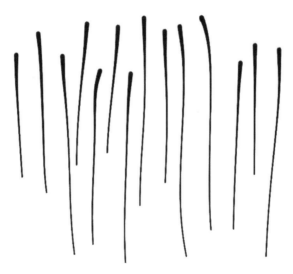

Throw lines - hold the pen like you are going to write as normal and place the nib on the page with your arm across your body. Imagine your wrist is attached to a zip line that you are resisting and then let go. Draw a horizontal line across the page. Repeat this several times. If you are doing it right you would get a fairly straight horizontal line that is thick at the beginning and then tapers off.

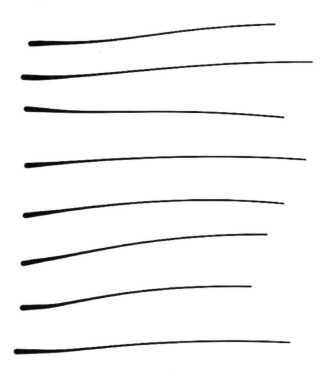

X Lines - like the previous two exercises but start across the body and draw diagonal lines bottom to top and top to bottom.

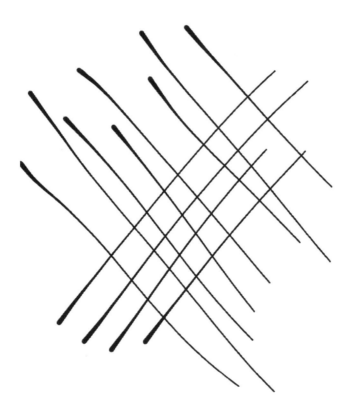

Handwriting

Fill two pages with the alphabet in upper case and repeat with lower case. Look critically at your handwriting. Find letters you like...for example the way you have drawn an "S" circle it. Repeat for any other letters you are happy with.

Now underline letters you are not so happy with...spend some time slowly writing them how you would like. Do a few lines of just one letter until you are happy.

Remember, you are not aiming for perfection.

LEGIBLE, REPEATABLE, FAST

Banners

Pick a banner style and draw it with the following headings at least 10 times each or until you are confident you can do it neatly and with speed. You can practice with these headings or any that you think would be in your regular repertoire.

Outcomes

Objectives

Introductions

Agenda

Teamwork

Leadership

Brainstorming

Words first then the box

Next steps

Follow up

Listening

You could listen to the news, or a TV show and practice capturing with words and pictures. You could also listen to TED talks and make charts of the key points, practicing headings handwriting, bullets and borders. TED talks are great because they are generally very short (between 3 and 17 minutes) and cover a range of interesting topics from the world of technology, education and design. www.ted.com

Visual Practice

Draw the following concepts using people or simple icons:

Leadership	Fun
Teamwork	Future
Strategy	Support
Knowledge	Learning
Communication	Teaching

Think of 10 words used in your work and come up with simple icons for each.

Sketch noting

You don't need to wait until you are presenting, training or facilitating. You can practice capturing content in words and pictures in any meeting.

Here is an example of notes I took on my iPad at a recent conference. The topic was "how to teach people to draw in 30 mins". These notes are for my benefit only, and a fun way to practice some techniques.

You can sketch note with pen and paper and if you want to use your iPad, I would suggest you download the app "Brushes".

Building your visual vocabulary

Begin with around 5 images you are really comfortable drawing, and then slowly build your vocabulary over time. Each of the following icons also have variations allowing you to use them for multiple different meanings or concepts.

The following pages provide worksheets for you to practice and develop your visual vocabulary.

My advice is to do one worksheet per week. By the end you could have over 50 new visual elements added to your vocabulary.

Book

Step 1 – 2 simple birds

Step 2 – connect the lines

Your practice

Add lines on the page

Add extra pages

Add a horizon line

Add throw lines

Person

Step 1 – the head

O

Step 2 – the body

Your practice

Make it a child

Add a horizon line

Give it a shadow

Add throw lines

Page

Step 1 – rectangle

Step 2 – add lines

Your practice

Put it at an angle

Turn up a corner

Add extra pages

Make a ring binder

Road

Step 1 – Horizon Line and road

Step 2 – Add lanes

Your practice

Add road signs

Head for the hills

Windy road

Add an aura

Flag

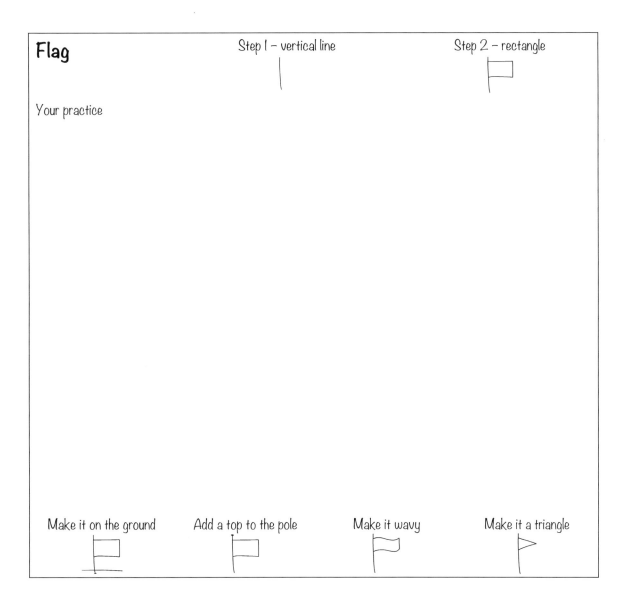

Step 1 – vertical line

Step 2 – rectangle

Your practice

Make it on the ground

Add a top to the pole

Make it wavy

Make it a triangle

Building

Step 1 – 3D Rectangle

Step 2 – Windows & door

Your practice

Add a horizon line

Add extra buildings

Add a flag

Add throw lines

Flipchart

Step 1 – rectangle

Step 2 – add legs

Your practice

Add a horizon line

Add words/lines

Add an extra page

Add throw lines

Globe

Step 1 – Circle

Step 2 – top and base

Your practice

Add a horizon line

Longitude and latitude

Continents

Continents with no base

Clock

Step 1 – circle

Step 2 – Hands

Your practice

Add number indicators

Make it more 3D

Add a horizon line

Give it a handle

Cloud

Step 1 – small and large fluffy sections

Step 2 – Close with a straight line

Your practice

Add rain

Add extra clouds

Make a storm

Put a person under

Bomb

Step 1 – circle

Step 2 – Fuse and fuse entry

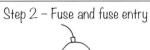

Your practice

Add a horizon line

Add a lit fuse

Add a word

Add a hand

Computer

Step 1 – Rectangle with stand

Step 2 – Keyboard

Your practice

Add a horizon line

Add a screen

Add a word

CONNECT

Add a mouse

Light globe

Step 1 – Tight Spring

Step 2 – Oval

Your practice

Add the element

Add a thought bubble

Add a switch

Add throw lines

Chapter 7

In conclusion

Nothing Ventured, Nothing Gained

Decide to do it – choose the right time

Get some **tools** – buy a nice set of pens

Develop your **skills** – practice using the drills

Have a **practice** run – get some paper on the wall and try some techniques relevant to your material

Capture content using sketch notes – at meetings, in front of the TV, when travelling on public transport.

5 Step Flipchart

1. Choose your colours (3-4)

2. Use a consistent heading style (Colour/ Banner/ Box)

3. Decide between a list (with bullet) or popcorn style (with visual element)

4. Add an icon/person/symbol

5. Draw a border around the whole thing

In my experience, trainers, facilitators and presenters watch and learn from others in their field, improve on ideas, then incorporate them into their work. I think this ok as long as you reference your source.

You have my permission to use EVERYTHING in this book for your own personal use, except Brandy Agerbeck's drawing. You need to contact her directly for that.

My permission extends to copying drawings or icons for your own flipcharts and feel free to mention me as your source in workshops, etc. If you publish anything, please reference.

Acknowledgements

A big THANK YOU:

To Maree Burgess, Rita Malvone,
Di Granger, Joanne Smith and Tracey Ezard
for proofreading the various iterations of
this book and providing invaluable feedback.

To Lynn Carruthers, Brandy Agerbeck and
Tomi Nagai-Rothe for being my teachers and
mentors in this space.

To David Sibbett and Guido Neuland for
being such inspirational leaders in our field by
pioneering the tools and techniques that
make us successful.

References & Resources

Visual Mojo by Lynne Cazaly

The Graphic Facilitators Guide by Brandy Agerbeck

Bikablo series via the Neuland website

The Back of the Napkin by Dan Roam

Draw Squad by Mark Kistler

Discovery Doodles by Diane Durand

Slide:ology by Nancy Duarte

Visual Meetings by David Sibbett

The Sketchnote Handbook by Mike Rohde

Charters Markers   Buy from www.grove.com

Neuland No. One ®   Buy from www.neuland.com

Neuland BigOne ®

fineOne by Neuland®

Mr Sketch Markers   Buy from OK Office Supplies

www. grove.com

www.neuland.com

www.ifvp.org

www.ted.com